Early Reader titles are ideal for children
existing phonics knowledge to practise re
sentences with help. Each book uses a sm
repeated and decodable words to steadily build reading confidence.

Special features:

Opening pages introduce key story words

Careful match between story and pictures

Large, clear type

Ladybird

Educational Consultants: Geraldine Taylor and James Clements
Book Banding Consultant: Kate Ruttle

LADYBIRD BOOKS

UK | USA | Canada | Ireland | Australia
India | New Zealand | South Africa

Ladybird Books is part of the Penguin Random House group of companies
whose addresses can be found at global.penguinrandomhouse.com.

www.penguin.co.uk   www.puffin.co.uk   www.ladybird.co.uk

Penguin
Random House
UK

Text adapted from *Peppa Pig: Fun at the Fair* first published by Ladybird Books Ltd 2011
Read It Yourself edition first published by Ladybird Books Ltd 2015
This edition published 2024
001

Printed in China

The authorized representative in the EEA is Penguin Random House Ireland,
Morrison Chambers, 32 Nassau Street, Dublin D02 YH68

A CIP catalogue record for this book is available from the British Library

ISBN: 978-0-241-56536-0

All correspondence to:
Ladybird Books
Penguin Random House Children's
One Embassy Gardens, 8 Viaduct Gardens, London SW11 7BW

Read It Yourself

Fun at the Fair

Adapted by Lorraine Horsley and Ellen Philpott

George

Mummy Pig

Peppa Pig

Daddy Pig

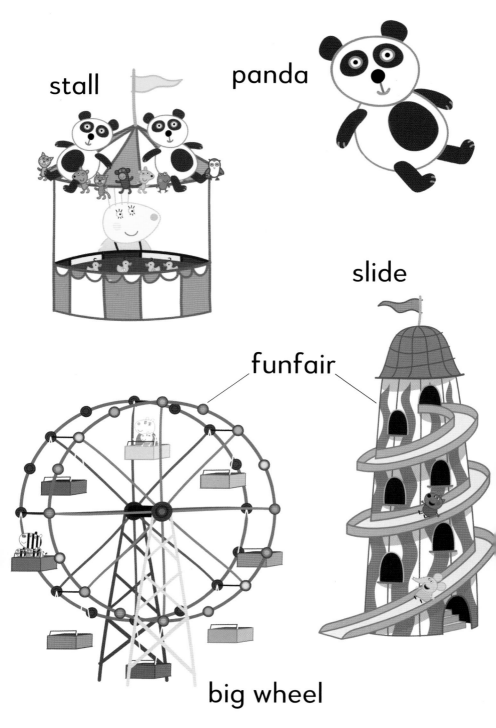

stall

panda

slide

funfair

big wheel

7

Peppa Pig, George,
Mummy and Daddy Pig
are at the funfair.

Peppa's friends
are all at the
funfair, too.

Peppa and Mummy Pig
go to the stalls.

"I love the big pandas,"
says Peppa.

Mummy Pig wins a big
panda from the stall.

"Hooray!" says Peppa.

13

George wants to have a go on the big slide.

Daddy Pig goes with him.

15

George loves the slide.

But the slide is too big
for Daddy Pig.

"I don't like this slide,"
he says.

Peppa and Mummy Pig
go to the next stall.

Mummy Pig wins another
big panda for Peppa.

19

George wants to go on
the big wheel next.

Daddy Pig goes
with him.

George loves the big wheel.

But the wheel is too big
for Daddy.

"I don't like this wheel,"
he says.

Now everyone is at the stalls.

Peppa wants Mummy Pig to win another panda.

25

Mummy Pig wins all the
pandas at the funfair!

"Hooray for Mummy!"
says Peppa.

27

Now Peppa's friends all
have a panda from Peppa.

"Hooray!" say Peppa's
friends.

Everyone loves funfairs!

29

How much do you remember about the story of *Peppa Pig: Fun at the Fair*? Answer these questions and find out!

- What does Mummy Pig win for Peppa?

- What do Daddy Pig and George go on first?

- Who does not like the big wheel?

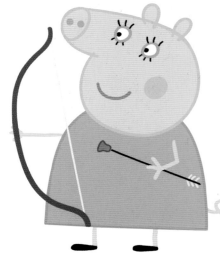